MARIE CURIE

Published by Creative Education
123 South Broad Street
Mankato, Minnesota 56001
Creative Education is an imprint of The Creative Company.

DESIGN AND PRODUCTION **EVANSDAY DESIGN**

PHOTOGRAPHS BY Corbis (Bettmann, Hulton-Deutsch Collection,
The Mariners' Museum, Setboun, Underwood & Underwood),
Getty Images (AFP, Hulton Archive, Henri Manuel/Hulton Archive)

"Autobiographical Notes" excerpt from *Pierre Curie*,
published in 1923 by The Macmillan Company.

LIBRARY OF CONGRESS CATALOGING-IN-PUBLICATION DATA
Healy, Nick.
Marie Curie / by Nick Healy.
p. cm. — (Genius)
ISBN 1-58341-332-4
1. Curie, Marie, 1867–1934–Juvenile literature. 2. Chemists–Poland–
Biography–Juvenile literature.
I. Title. II. Genius (Mankato, Minn.)

QD22.C8H36 2004
540'.92–dc22   2004056167

First edition

9 8 7 6 5 4 3 2 1

[M A R I E   C U R I E]

GENIUS

Nick Healy

MARIE CURIE CHANGED THE WAY THE WORLD THOUGHT ABOUT SCIENCE,

BUT SHE COULD HAVE ACCOMPLISHED NOTHING IF SHE HAD NOT

FIRST IGNORED THE WAY THE WORLD THOUGHT ABOUT HER. FROM

HER EARLIEST DAYS, CURIE FACED OPPRESSION AND DISCRIMINA-

TION, AND SHE HAD TO JOURNEY ALONG TRAILS NEVER BEFORE

TRAVELED BY A WOMAN. YET SHE MOVED THOUGH LIFE WITH A

CALMNESS AND MODESTY THAT MADE IT ALL APPEAR INEVITABLE.

SHE NEVER STOPPED SEEKING KNOWLEDGE, EVEN WHEN HER WORK

WEAKENED AND SCARRED HER BODY. HER RESEARCH—MUCH OF

IT CONDUCTED IN A COLD, DAMP SHED BEHIND HER HUSBAND'S

SCHOOL—CHALLENGED SOME OF THE MOST BASIC IDEAS ABOUT

THE NATURE OF MATTER. HER FINDINGS OPENED NEW PATHS OF

DISCOVERY IN WHAT CAME TO BE KNOWN AS THE NUCLEAR AGE.

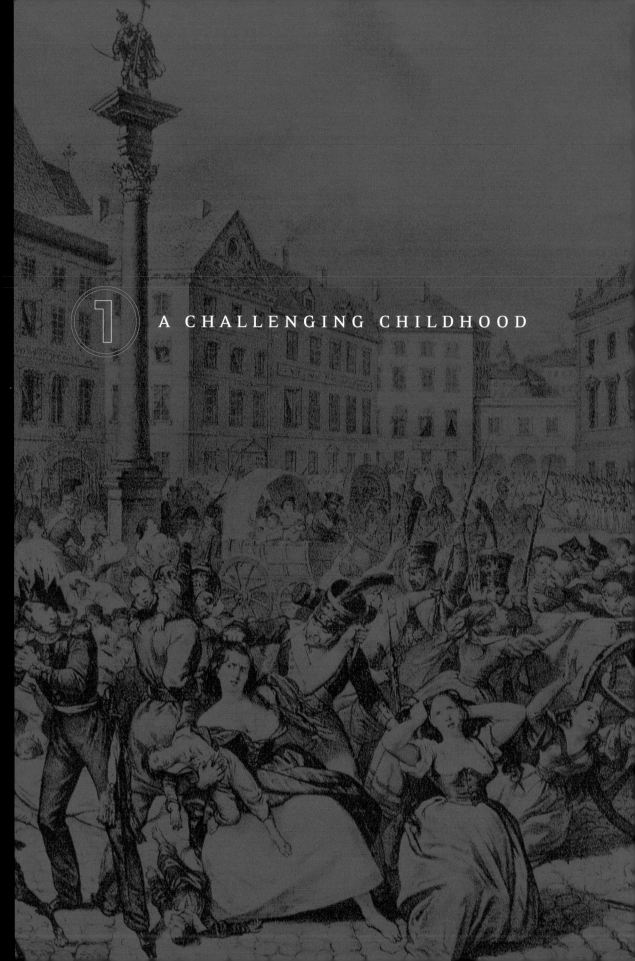

1 A CHALLENGING CHILDHOOD

TO APPRECIATE THE LIFE OF MARIE CURIE, IT IS NECESSARY TO UNDERSTAND THE TIME AND PLACE SHE WAS BORN. HER BIRTH, ON NOVEMBER 7, 1867, OCCURRED IN THE TROUBLED POLISH CITY OF WARSAW. NEIGHBORING COUNTRIES HAD LONG SINCE OVERRUN POLAND, ONCE THE LARGEST NATION IN EUROPE.

From youth, Manya was a superior student

Russia ruled Warsaw and a large share of Polish territory, and did so with little regard for the people and their traditions. To be a Pole, simply to speak the Polish language, required a willingness to challenge authority and to stubbornly cling to dreams of a better future. If Marie had not taken on those traits, the world might have been deprived of her great mind.

Marie was born Manya Sklodowska. Her name sometimes appears in books as "Marya," but she was known by Manya until she left Poland at age 24. The youngest of five children, Manya grew up in a home where learning was valued. Her parents, Wladislaw and Bronislawa, were teachers, and both believed education provided hope for Poles. An attempt to rebel against Russian rule had failed several years before Manya's birth, and many Poles adopted a new approach to resistance called "positivism." They believed that learning and enlightenment—not a violent uprising—would lead to freedom.

Teaching provided a comfortable way of life for Manya's family. Her father taught mathematics and physics at a government-run high school, where he worked under the watchful eye of Russian administrators. Teaching Polish language and history was forbidden, and Wladislaw's supervisors enforced strict control over what went on in the classroom. Manya's mother, on the other hand, was the director of a private school for girls, where there was less interference. Still, Russian inspectors checked in to make sure students were learning Russian history and language, not their own.

Manya's education began early, and her dazzling intelligence showed itself immediately. Her parents expected their children to learn to read before they entered school, but even they were surprised when four-year-old Manya snatched up a book and began reading entire sentences aloud. Most children her age had not yet learned the alphabet. Later, Manya was known to memorize entire poems after hearing them just once. Her sisters and brother also were excellent students, and the whole family fostered the learning of its youngest member.

Sadly, several misfortunes rocked the hopeful spirit in Manya's home. Her father lost his teaching job, and the family fell into financial despair. They were forced to take in boarders, whom her father tutored. Manya slept in the dining room, and each morning, she had to wake early and put away her bedding to make way for boarders expecting breakfast. Some people believe that this crowded environment contributed to a tragedy that hit the family in 1876, when Manya's eldest sister, Zosia, died

"Marie Curie is, of all celebrated beings, the only one whom fame has not corrupted."

ALBERT EINSTEIN
LEGENDARY PHYSICIST

Timeline **1876**   TYPHOID CLAIMS THE LIFE OF MANYA'S SISTER ZOSIA.

The Sklodowska sisters, Manya (left) and Bronia, made a deal to support each other while taking turns pursuing higher education in Paris.

of typhoid. The final blow came two years later, when Manya's mother died of tuberculosis.

Soon after her mother's death, Manya began classes at a public school called Gymnasium Number Three. The school suffered from scarce resources, and Russian teachers treated their Polish students with suspicion and disrespect. Manya later called the environment "altogether unbearable," but she devoted herself to her studies and thrived. At age 15, she graduated as the top student in her class. She had worked so hard, however, that she was mentally exhausted and physically weak.

Manya recovered by taking a year to relax. She relished the chance to visit relatives, attend dances, and bask in her youth—happily declaring that "never again, never in my whole life, will I have such fun." Many Polish girls her age expected to marry and begin a family. Manya, however, aspired to a different sort of life, and she stubbornly held on to other dreams.

Her sister Bronia shared her desire to leave behind Russian rule and pursue higher education in Paris. The trouble was neither could afford to make the move. Their only hope was to help each other, so the sisters made a deal. Bronia would leave to study medicine in Paris, and Manya would go to work to support her older sister. When Bronia finished school, the deal would be reversed, with Bronia supporting Manya during her studies. At last Manya's goal seemed possible, but she had to be patient.

MANYA GRADUATES FROM GYMNASIUM NUMBER THREE AND IS FIRST IN HER CLASS.   *Timeline* **1883**

The strength that propelled her to greatness even in the face of personal hardship is evident in Manya's determined expression.

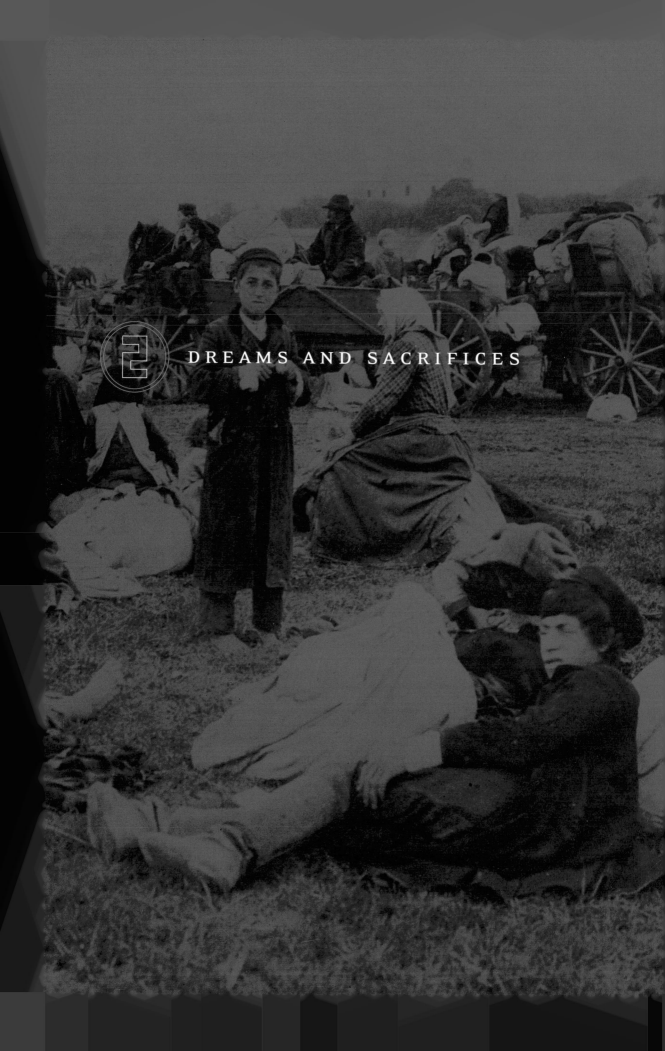

DREAMS AND SACRIFICES

IN 1886, MANYA WENT TO WORK AS A GOVERN-
ESS, OR LIVE-IN BABYSITTER. SHE WORKED ABOUT 60
MILES (100 KM) OUTSIDE WARSAW ON THE SUCCESSFUL
SUGAR BEET FARM OF THE ZORAWSKI FAMILY. HER DU-
TIES FILLED HER DAYS FROM DAWN TO DUSK. SHE WAS
A TUTOR FOR THE ZORAWSKI CHILDREN AND A SERVANT
TO THE ENTIRE HOUSEHOLD. WITH THE PERMISSION
OF HER EMPLOYER, SHE ALSO TAUGHT PEASANT CHIL-
DREN WHO LIVED NEARBY HOW TO READ AND WRITE.

Manya longed to learn in an educational setting

Her life in the country was difficult. However, living with the Zorawskis meant all her expenses were paid, and she could send more of her wages to Bronia than if she had stayed in Warsaw.

Manya made good use of her meager amount of free time. She continued to study on her own and challenged herself by read-ing the most important literary and scientific works of the time. She read on a wide variety of subjects, but her interest began to focus on mathematics and physics. The isolation of rural living frustrated Manya. She yearned to be in a formal school setting, with learned instructors to guide her and laboratory space for her experiments.

A great disappointment also marked Manya's time as a rural gov-erness. She fell in love with the Zorawskis' eldest son, Kazimierz, who was a mathematics student at the University of Warsaw. They

MANYA IS HIRED AS A GOVERNESS FOR A RURAL POLISH FAMILY.   *Timeline* 1886

met when he was home on vacation, and she hoped they would be married. His parents, however, did not believe a lowly governess would be a proper wife for their son, and Kazimierz went along with their wishes. Manya sank into despair, even questioning her dreams and ambitions. To make matters worse, she had to remain with the Zorawskis until her contract was fulfilled. Only then, at age 22, could she return to Warsaw, where she again found work as a governess and bided her time.

As Bronia neared the completion of her studies in 1890, she became engaged to a fellow medical student. In a letter home, Bronia invited Manya to live with her and her husband in Paris. The opportunity Manya had so long desired had finally come. Still, she struggled with the decision she now faced. Leaving behind her father would be difficult. In a letter to her sister, Manya wrote, "I want to give him a little happiness in his old age. On the other hand, my heart breaks when I think of ruining my abilities, which must have been worth, anyhow, something." After a year of uncertainty, Manya finally left for Paris.

Paris was a lively and exciting city, where the Eiffel Tower had risen into the skyline just two years earlier. Manya went to live with her sister as planned but soon found the home too filled with distractions. She had come to study at the Sorbonne, part of the University of Paris, and wanted nothing to interfere with her work. She left her sister's home and took a small sixth-floor apartment near the university.

Timeline **1891**   MANYA MOVES TO PARIS TO STUDY AT THE SORBONNE, WHERE SHE USES THE NAME "MARIE SKLODOWSKA."

The Sorbonne was founded in 1257 in Paris, and an impressive list of philosophers, writers, scientists, and theologians have studied there; for Manya, it was heaven.

On November 5, 1891, Manya enrolled as "Marie Sklodowska" at the Sorbonne, where she joined about 200 women studying alongside 9,000 men. Her French was less than perfect. She had not studied in a formal school setting since she was 15. She had little money. Still, she couldn't have been happier.

Marie thrived at the Sorbonne. After two years, she graduated first in her class with the equivalent of a master's degree in physics. She also won a scholarship to continue studying for another year, and in 1894, she received a similar degree for mathematics, finishing second in her class. That same year, she met Pierre Curie, and a great romantic and scientific partnership began.

MARIE MARRIES PIERRE CURIE AND TAKES THE NAME "MARIE CURIE." Timeline **1895**

Marie met Pierre Curie in Paris, and the couple married a year later; they would go on to form one of the greatest partnerships science had ever known.

A MEETING OF MINDS

MARIE FIRST ENCOUNTERED PIERRE CURIE AT THE HOME OF A POLISH PHYSICIST. THEY WERE FASCINATED WITH EACH OTHER. SHE SAW IN HIM "A DREAMER ABSORBED IN HIS REFLECTIONS," AND HE SAW A COOL-EYED WOMAN WITH A BRILLIANT MIND. MARIE GAVE HIM HER ADDRESS THAT DAY, THOUGH IT WAS CONSIDERED IMPROPER BEHAVIOR FOR A LADY OF THE TIME. SOON THEY HAD DINNER TOGETHER, AND THEIR RELATIONSHIP BLOOMED.

Marie and Pierre at work together

Pierre Curie, who at 35 was eight years Marie's senior, was already an accomplished scientist. His background was unusual, as much of his education had been informal, but he and his brother, Jacques, had made important discoveries together. They studied electricity, magnetism, heat, and crystals. They were the first to find that some crystals generate electrical current when compressed, a phenomenon they named piezoelectricity. The brothers also invented the electrometer, a device that measured electricity given off by crystals and other types of matter. Their ideas are still in use today in devices such as mobile phones and quartz watches.

Marie and Pierre were married in 1895, and they celebrated by bicycling through northern France. Their return to Paris began a very busy, productive time in their lives. Marie was preparing to take an exam that would make her a licensed teacher; Pierre was preparing his dissertation to complete a doctoral degree. Pierre was appointed a professor at *Ecole Municipale de Physique et Chimie Industrielle* (Municipal College of Physics and Industrial Chemistry), or EPCI, in Paris. He had been a laboratory director at the school for more than a decade. Marie earned her license to teach, finishing first in her class once again.

Marie soon discovered she would have to meet two sets of demands in her life. She was a working woman in a world that didn't recognize that as an option, and she was a wife expected to manage a household like other women. Research and laboratory work were conducted almost exclusively by men, yet Marie persisted in her experiments. She maintained this balancing act even when she became pregnant and gave birth to a daughter, Irene, in 1897. Pierre's father, whose wife had recently died, came to help with the baby, and Marie pursued a doctoral degree of her own.

Her research for her dissertation led Marie to discoveries that amazed the scientific world and made her famous. She decided to study the mysterious energy, or rays, emitted by a metallic element called uranium. Working in a rundown shed at EPCI, she searched for other materials that emitted rays as uranium did. Then she began to examine the traits of these materials and to observe how they changed under different conditions. Her research advanced quickly; one discovery led to another. Soon Pierre abandoned his own research into magnetism to join Marie in her work.

"I was very much under the influence of my mother, whom I loved and profoundly admired, and could not throughout my childhood conceive of her having any human failings. I was quite different from her, however, being more like my father. This may be one of the reasons why we got on so well."

IRENE JOLIOT-CURIE
MARIE'S OLDER DAUGHTER AND
NOBEL PRIZE-WINNING SCIENTIST

Timeline **1898** THE CURIES PUBLISH PAPERS ON POLONIUM AND RADIUM. THEY COIN THE TERM "RADIOACTIVE."

In addition to the discoveries and awards their scientific work generated, Marie and Pierre's marriage produced daughters Irene (left) and her younger sister Eve (right).

The Curies were able to identify a new element that gave off rays at a much greater level than uranium. They called this new metal polonium, in honor of Marie's homeland of Poland. In their July 1898 article describing the discovery of polonium, the Curies also coined the term "radioactive" to describe substances that emitted rays, or radiation.

In December 1898, they published another article describing a second new and highly radioactive element called radium. Although they had identified radium, they had not yet obtained a pure sample of it. This turned out to be a huge undertaking, requiring tons of radioactive material and years of work. In time, Pierre shifted his interest to the properties of radioactive emissions, but Marie continued to work on radium. Finally, in 1902, Marie isolated a tiny amount—0.1 gram—of pure radium. The element gave off so much energy that it glowed blue-green and became hot.

The years 1898 to 1902 were the busiest and, according to Marie, the happiest in the couple's lives. Each published several papers describing their many discoveries. They won awards for their research. Marie became the first female instructor at France's best women's teacher training school. When she completed her doctoral work in 1903, the examination committee declared her discoveries to be the greatest scientific achievement ever contained in a dissertation. Later that year, Marie and her husband were awarded the Nobel Prize for Physics, which they shared with French physicist Henri Becquerel.

THE CURIES' SECOND DAUGHTER, EVE, IS BORN. Timeline 1904

Marie felt quite at home in her laboratory and spent much time with her husband there; in 1898, the Curies identified two new elements: polonium and radium.

OPENING THE NUCLEAR AGE

PERHAPS MARIE CURIE'S SINGLE GREATEST CON-
TRIBUTION TO SCIENCE CAME AMID THE FLURRY OF
DISCOVERIES SHE AND HER HUSBAND MADE IN 1898.
THAT YEAR, THE CURIES PUBLISHED TWO SIGNIFI-
CANT PAPERS. THE FIRST EXPLAINED THE DISCOV-
ERY OF POLONIUM AND MARKED THE FIRST TIME
THE WORD "RADIOACTIVE" WAS USED. THE SEC-
OND PAPER REVEALED THE DISCOVERY OF RADIUM.

It also explained radioactivity as an atomic property—something occurring within nature's smallest building block—of matter. This statement helped launch a new direction in science that ultimately led, for better or worse, to the unleashing of nuclear energy's enormous power.

The research Marie began as preparation for her doctoral disser-tation followed on the heels of recent discoveries made by other scientists. Two years earlier, a German physicist named Wilhelm Roentgen had discovered the X-ray. Roentgen had been experi-menting with a vacuum tube known as a cathode-ray tube. It was understood that sending electrical current through a cathode-ray tube produced light. But Roentgen discovered that when the tube was covered in light-blocking material, invisible rays still escaped. These rays could pass through materials such as paper or skin but were blocked by some metals and hard substances such as bone.

German physicist Wilhelm Roentgen

He noticed that the invisible rays also produced a strange glow when they contacted certain materials. Roentgen called them "X-rays" because he could not explain their nature.

Soon Henri Becquerel, the French physicist who later shared a Nobel Prize with the Curies, attempted to build on the discovery of X-rays. Becquerel studied materials known to give off light when exposed to sunlight. He wondered if those materials also gave off X-rays. In testing a metallic element called uranium, he found it gave off invisible rays whether or not it was exposed to sunlight. Roentgen's X-rays were produced through an electrical effect, but the rays coming off uranium seemed to happen naturally. The source of the rays, or the energy that drove them, was a mystery.

Marie attempted to find out more about these strange rays. X-rays and the rays described by Becquerel shared an important trait: both made the air around them carry electricity. That meant Marie could use the electrometer invented by Pierre and his brother in her search for other materials that emitted rays. She quickly found that a material called thorium also made such emissions. The electrometer also helped her discover a key trait of these mysterious rays. She found that the energy given off by uranium did not change, regardless of the substance's form or external conditions. It did not matter if the uranium was pure or mixed with other materials. It did not matter if it was cold or hot, solid or gas. The level of energy emitted depended only on the amount of uranium present.

"There were several elements in pitchblende, but one of them was radium, which turned out to be enormously radioactive, and that was important because the radioactivity provided clues to the nature of matter and really opened the door of the nuclear age."

SUSAN QUINN
JOURNALIST AND BIOGRAPHER

Timeline 1906   PIERRE CURIE DIES AFTER BEING STRUCK BY A HORSE-DRAWN CARRIAGE. MARIE TAKES OVER HIS TEACHING JOB AT THE SORBONNE.

Henri Becquerel shared the 1903 Nobel Prize with the Curies and worked closely with Marie in studying the effects of X-rays.

This discovery spurred many others. Marie found that pitch-blende ore gave off far more energy than uranium or any other element was known to emit. She realized another substance had to be present, and this conclusion led to the discovery of polonium and radium. Her paper describing radium also gave Marie the chance to explain the most important idea to come from her research. Radioactivity, she found, was not the product of a chemical reaction, and it did not depend upon influences such as heat or light. It also did not depend upon how atoms were arranged. Rather, radioactivity came from inside the atom.

One reason the discovery of radium was so important was that a tiny amount of it produced a great amount of energy. A powerful force existed inside its atoms, a force that had previously been beyond imagination. Two centuries earlier, English scientist Isaac Newton had described atoms as tiny, hard particles—like little balls. In the 1890s, Newton's idea had already been challenged. The discovery of the electron showed that particles smaller than the atom existed.

Marie's research blew away Newton's vision of the atom and changed the way scientists thought about the atom. Her findings helped other scientists discover the true structure of the atom. Her research also led others to see the atom as something unstable and changeable. And there began the path that led to all discoveries about atomic energy and its uses, from nuclear power plants to nuclear bombs.

DURING WORLD WAR I, MARIE OUTFITS X-RAY SITES AND X-RAY TRUCKS, AND SHE TRAINS STAFF TO OPERATE THEM. *Timeline* **1914–18**

*Marie's work helped lead to the creation of the atomic bomb, which would
be used by the U.S. against Japan years later to help end World War II.*

TRAGEDY AND PERSEVERANCE

FILLED MARIE'S LIFE IN THE YEARS AFTER THE DISCOVERY OF RADIUM. THE TASK OF ISOLATING PURE RADIUM TURNED OUT TO BE BRUTAL, EXHAUSTING WORK. STARTING WITH TONS OF PITCHBLENDE, MARIE PERFORMED CHEMICAL SEPARATION PROCESSES ON LARGE AMOUNTS OF MATERIAL. BY 1903, THE WORK WAS TAKING A TOLL ON THE CURIES. WHEN THEY WON THE NOBEL PRIZE, BOTH WERE TOO ILL TO TRAVEL TO SWEDEN FOR THE AWARD CEREMONY.

Marie and other scientists experimenting with radium

They did not know it, but the Curies were suffering because of exposure to radiation.

They routinely handled radioactive substances without protection. Pierre was known to keep a tube of radium in his coat pocket, so he could show friends the strange, glowing substance. He often explained that radium was one million times more radioactive than uranium. Marie kept radium salts, giving off their blue-green light, at her bedside. The Curies experienced pain and scaling of the skin on their hands, along with fatigue and weakness, but Marie chalked up their problems to overwork.

After winning the Nobel Prize, Marie was likely the world's most famous scientist. The fact that a women was at the forefront of such important work grabbed the attention of newspapers. And Marie's discovery—that glowing substance with mysterious powers—fascinated people in all walks of life. Still, she had never received a salary for her work as a researcher. That changed in 1904 when the Sorbonne chose to make Pierre a professor, and Marie became his assistant. The couple's second daughter, Eve, was born that same year.

A great tragedy shook Marie's life two years later. After attending a luncheon for professors of science, Pierre set off on foot through the streets of Paris. Opening his umbrella as he dodged the rain, he stepped into the path of a horse-drawn wagon. The driver pulled the reins, but it was too late. Pierre fell under the wheels and was crushed.

Soon after her husband's death, Marie returned to the laboratory. At work, she found relief, or at least distraction, from the sadness of her life. Eventually she was appointed to fill her late husband's job at the Sorbonne. Her first lecture came 15 years after she had arrived at the school as a student. She became the first female professor in France, and her new rank provided a good salary to support her family.

Marie won a second Nobel Prize in 1911, this one for chemistry. But it was small consolation in a year marked by hardships. Early in 1911, she was a candidate for election to the French Academy of Sciences, a powerful organization made up entirely of men. Her candidacy became the focus of great attention, and some people fought bitterly against having a woman join the academy. Despite her qualifications, Marie lost by two votes. She suffered further humiliation when a scandal arose over her relationship with scientist Paul Langevin, a married man who had left his wife.

"It is complicated because they did not think of her as a thinker, but they did not think of her as a woman either—because a woman must not think and a thinker must not be a woman!"

FRANCOISE BALIBAR
A PHYSICS PROFESSOR AT
PARIS UNIVERSITY

Timeline **1921**   MARIE MAKES HER FIRST TRIP TO AMERICA.

Marie continued to perform experiments through scandals and failing health; she is shown here in her laboratory at the University of Paris.

> "I feel the need to tell you how much
> I have come to admire your spirit,
> your energy, and your honesty….
> If the rabble continues to be occu-
> pied with you, simply stop reading
> that drivel. Leave it to the vipers
> it was fabricated for."
>
> ALBERT EINSTEIN
> IN A LETTER TO MARIE

Under intense criticism and pressure, Marie became quite ill and departed to recover in England.

Marie endured and still had many contributions to make. She oversaw the creation of the Radium Institute in Paris, which opened in 1914. The outbreak of World War I delayed her plans for research at the institute, and Marie joined the war effort. She organized a fleet of 20 X-ray ambulances and arranged for X-ray equipment at 200 stationary locations. She and her daughter Irene even traveled to the front to help treat wounded soldiers. After the war, Marie returned to her work and devoted great energy to the Radium Institute. With help from her friend Missy Meloney, an American journalist, Marie twice traveled to the United States on fundraising trips. She received a hero's welcome, met with presidents, and raised thousands of dollars.

By the mid-1920s, scientists recognized the dangers of radioactivity. People who worked with radium and other radioactive materials suffered a wide range of problems, from burns to anemia to cancer. Marie experienced a great deal of pain and illness in the years before her death on July 4, 1934. She died from leukemia, and the official cause of her disease was "a long accumulation of radiations." She was 66.

MARIE DIES ON JULY 4 AT THE AGE OF 66 AT A SANITARIUM IN THE FRENCH ALPS. *Timeline* 1934

Irene Joliot-Curie (pictured) followed in the footsteps of her mother and won the 1937 Nobel Prize for the discovery of artificial radioactivity.

35

WORDS

WHEN MARIE CURIE WROTE A BIOGRAPHY OF HER

LATE HUSBAND, SHE DID IT WITH HESITATION. IN THE

PREFACE TO *PIERRE CURIE*, PUBLISHED IN 1923, SHE SAYS

SHE HAD HOPED THAT SOMEONE WHO HAD KNOWN HIM

IN HIS YOUTH—PERHAPS HIS BROTHER, JACQUES—WOULD

HAVE UNDERTAKEN THE TASK. BUT AS NO ONE STEPPED

FORWARD, SHE DECIDED TO GO AHEAD, TO "CONSERVE

HIS MEMORY" AND TO "REMIND THOSE WHO KNEW

HIM OF THE REASONS FOR WHICH THEY LOVED HIM."

AT THE BACK OF THE BOOK, THE PUBLISHER INCLUDED MARIE'S "AUTOBIOGRAPHICAL NOTES," WHICH SHE HAD BEEN EQUALLY HESITANT TO WRITE. IN HER INTRODUCTION, MARIE REVEALS THAT SHE WAS PERSUADED TO INCLUDE HER OWN STORY BY "AMERICAN FRIENDS" AND THAT THE IDEA SEEMED "ALIEN" AT FIRST. SHE PROMISES THAT HER NOTES DESCRIBE ONLY THE "GENERAL COURSE AND ESSENTIAL FEATURES" OF HER LIFE, AND ARE NOT A "COMPLETE EXPRESSION OF PERSONAL FEELINGS." NONETHELESS, THE FOLLOWING EXCERPT PROVIDES INSIGHT INTO CRUCIAL MOMENTS OF HER LIFE. (EACH OF THE THREE SECTIONS APPEARS UNDER A TITLE ADDED TO PROVIDE CONTEXT FOR READERS.)

ARRIVING AT THE SORBONNE *So it was in November 1891, at the age of 24, that I was able to realize the dream that had always been present in my mind for several years.*

When I arrived in Paris I was affectionately welcomed by my sister and brother-in-law, but I stayed with them only for a few months, for they lived in one of the outside quarters of Paris where my brother-in-law was beginning a medical practice, and I needed to get nearer to the schools. I was finally installed, like many other students of my country, in a modest little room for which I gathered some furniture. I kept to this way of living during the four years of my student life.

It would be impossible to tell of all the good these years brought me. Undistracted by any outside occupation, I was entirely absorbed in the joy of learning and understanding. Yet, all the while, my living conditions were far from easy, my own funds being small and my family not having the means to aid me as they would have liked to do. However, my situation was not exceptional; it was the familiar experience of many of the Polish students whom I knew. The room I lived in was in a garret [an attic room, under a sloped roof], very cold in winter, for it was insufficiently heated by a small stove which often lacked coal. During a particularly rigorous winter, it was not unusual for the water to freeze in the basin in the night; to be able to sleep I was obliged to pile all my clothes on the bedcovers. In the same room I prepared my meals with the aid of an alcohol lamp and a few kitchen utensils. These meals were often reduced to bread with a cup of chocolate, eggs or fruit. I had no help in housekeeping and I myself carried the little coal I used up the six flights.

This life, painful from certain points of view, had, for all that, a real charm for me. It gave me a very precious sense of liberty and independence. Unknown in Paris, I was lost in the great city, but the feeling of living there alone, taking care of myself without any aid, did not at all depress me. If sometimes I felt lonesome, my usual state of mind was one of calm and great moral satisfaction.

All my mind was centered on my studies, which, especially at the beginning, were difficult. In fact, I was insufficiently prepared to follow the physical science course at the Sorbonne, for, despite all my efforts, I had not succeeded in acquiring in Poland a preparation as complete as that of the French students following the same course. So I was obliged to supply this deficiency, especially in mathematics. I divided my time between courses, experimental work, and study in the library. In the evening I worked in my room, sometimes very late into the night. All that I saw and learned that was new delighted me. It was like a new world opened to me, the world of science, which I was at last permitted to know in all liberty....

LIFE AS NEWLYWEDS   *With my marriage there began for me a new existence entirely different from the solitary life that I had known during the preceding years. My husband and I were so closely united by our affection and our common work that we passed nearly all of our time together. I have only a few letters from him, for we were so little apart. My husband spent all the time he could spare from his teaching at his research work in the laboratory of the school in which he was professor and I obtained authorization to work with him.*

Our living apartment was near the school, so we lost little time in going and coming. As our material resources were limited, I was obliged to attend to most of the housekeeping myself, particularly the preparation of meals. It was not easy to reconcile these household duties with my scientific work, yet, with good will, I managed it. The great thing was that we were alone together in the little home which gave us a peace and intimacy that were very enjoyable for us.

At the same time that I was working in the laboratory, I still had to take a few study courses, for I had decided to take part in the examination for a certificate that would allow me to teach young girls. If I succeeded in this,

I would be entitled to be named professor. In August 1896, after having devoted several months to preparation, I came out first in the examination.

Our principal distraction from the close work of the laboratory consisted in walks or bicycle rides in the country. My husband greatly enjoyed the out-of-doors and took great interest in the plants and animals of woods and meadows. Hardly a corner in the vicinity of Paris was unknown to him. I also loved the country and these excursions were a great joy for me as well as to him, relieving our mind from the tension of the scientific work. We used to bring home bunches of flowers. Sometimes we forgot all about the time and got back late at night….

PROVING THE EXISTENCE OF RADIUM   The School of Physics could give us no suitable premises, but for lack of anything better, the director permitted us to use an abandoned shed which had been in service as a dissecting room of the School of Medicine. Its glass roof did not afford complete shelter against rain; the heat was suffocating in summer, and the bitter cold of winter was only a little lessened by the iron stove, except in its immediate vicinity. There was no question of obtaining the needed proper apparatus in common use by chemists. We simply had some old pine-wood tables with furnaces and gas burners. We had to use the adjoining yard for those of our chemical operations that involved producing irritating gases; even then the gas often filled our shed. With this equipment we entered on our exhausting work.

Yet it was in this miserable old shed that we passed the best and happiest years of our life, devoting our entire days to our work. Often I had to prepare our lunch in the shed, so as not to interrupt some particularly important operation. Sometimes I had to spend a whole day mixing a boiling mass with a heavy iron rod nearly as large as myself. I would be broken with fatigue at the day's end. Other days, on the contrary, the work would be a most minute and delicate fractional crystallization, in the effort to concentrate the radium. I was then annoyed by the floating dust of iron and coal from which I could not protect my precious products. But I shall never be able to express the joy of the untroubled quietness of this atmosphere of research and the excitement of actual progress with the confident hope of still better results. The feeling of discouragement that sometimes came after some unsuccessful toil did not last long and gave way to renewed activity. We had happy moments devoted to a quiet discussion of our work, walking around our shed.

One of our joys was to go into our workroom at night; we then perceived on all sides the feebly luminous silhouettes of the bottles or capsules containing our products. It was really a lovely sight and one always new to us. The glowing tubes looked like faint, fairy lights.

Thus the months passed, and our efforts, hardly interrupted by short vacations, brought forth more and more complete evidence. Our faith grew ever stronger, and our work being more and more known, we found means to get new quantities of raw material and to carry on some of our crude processes in a factory, allowing me to give more time to the delicate finishing treatment.

At this stage I devoted myself especially to the purification of the radium, my husband being absorbed by the study of the physical properties of the rays emitted by the new substances. It was only after testing one ton of pitchblende residues that I could get definite results. Indeed we know today that even in the best minerals there are not more than a few decigrams of radium in a ton of raw material.

At last the time came when the isolated substances showed all the [characteristics] of a pure chemical body.... It had taken me almost four years to produce the kind of evidence which chemical science demands, that radium is truly a new element. One year would probably have been enough for the same purpose, if reasonable means had been at my disposal. The demonstration that cost so much effort was the basis of the new science of radioactivity....

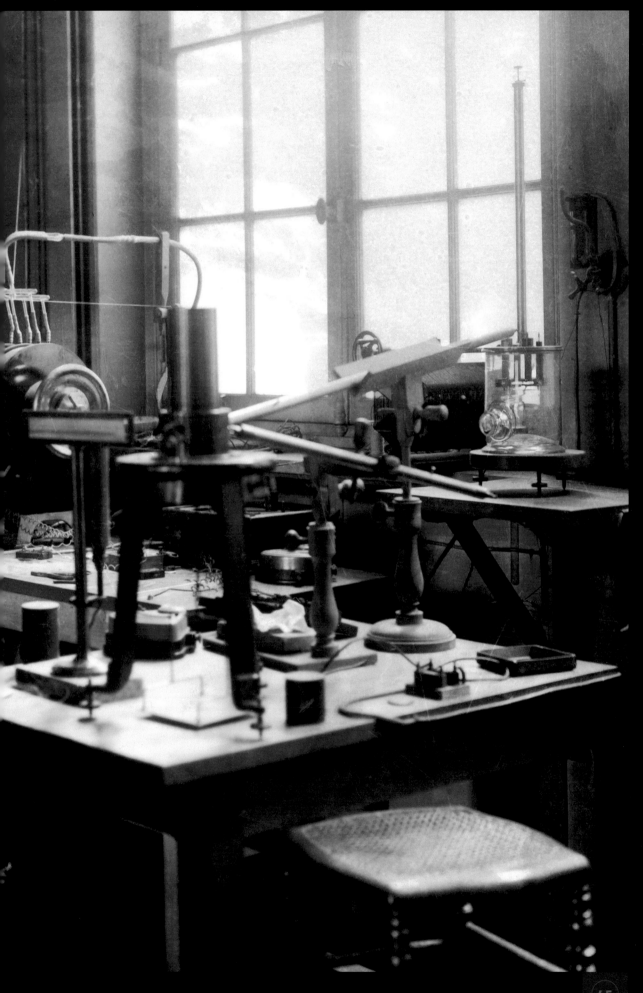

ACADEMY OF SCIENCES An admired and elite panel of French scientists whose members presented their research to the group and published in the academy's journal, the most prestigious scientific publication in France.

ATOMS The tiny parts that make up all forms of matter; atoms are made up of even smaller particles called protons, neutrons, and electrons.

ELEMENT A pure substance composed of identical atoms. Elements cannot be reduced to simpler substances by normal chemical means. All atoms in an element are the same, and they are unlike all other elements.

ISAAC NEWTON An English mathematician and physicist who, in the mid-1660s, laid the foundation for modern science through his discoveries on gravity, motion, and light.

LEUKEMIA A common form of cancer that starts in blood-forming tissue such as bone marrow and affects the production of blood cells.

MARIE "MISSY" MELONEY An American journalist and editor who befriended Marie Curie in the 1920s. She organized a lecture tour in the United States that helped Marie raise money for the Radium Institute.

NOBEL PRIZE A prestigious annual award that honors great achievements in physics, chemistry, medicine, literature, and the cause of peace.

PITCHBLENDE A brown to black mineral with a distinctive luster that is the chief ore-mineral source of uranium. It also contains small amounts of radium, thorium, polonium, lead, and helium.

POSITIVISM A political movement popular in the late 1800s in Poland. Positivism centered on a belief that through knowledge, enlightenment, and science people could overcome oppression.

TUBERCULOSIS An infection that attacks the lungs and other body parts, and causes violent coughing and breathing difficulties.

TYPHOID A disease caused by a bacterial infection that attacks the digestive system. It is transmitted from person to person through food or drinking water, and it is therefore mainly hygiene and sanitary conditions that determine its spread.

WILHELM ROENTGEN A scientist who discovered X-rays while working as a professor at the University of Würzburg in Germany. He won the Nobel Prize for Physics in 1901.